Math Counts

Time

Children's Press®

An Imprint of Scholastic Inc.

About This Series

In keeping with the major goals of the National Council of Teachers of Mathematics, children will become mathematical problem solvers, learn to communicate mathematically, and learn to reason mathematically by using the series Math Counts.

Pattern, Shape, and *Size* may be investigated first—in any sequence.

Sorting, Counting, and *Numbers* may be used next, followed by *Time, Length, Weight,* and *Capacity.*

—Ramona G. Choos, Professor of Mathematics,
Senior Adviser to the Dean of Continuing Education, Chicago State University;
Sponsor for Chicago Elementary Teachers' Mathematics Club

Author's Note

Mathematics is a part of a child's world. It is not only interpreting numbers or mastering tricks of addition or multiplication. Mathematics is about ideas. These ideas have been developed to explain particular qualities such as size, weight, and height, as well as relationships and comparisons. Yet all too often the important part that an understanding of mathematics will play in a child's development is forgotten or ignored.

Most adults can solve simple mathematical tasks without the need for counters, beads, or fingers. Young children find such abstractions almost impossible to master. They need to see, talk, touch, and experiment.

The photographs and text in these books have been chosen to encourage talk about topics that are essentially mathematical. By talking, the young reader can explore some of the central concepts that support mathematics. It is on an understanding of these concepts that a student's future mastery of mathematics will be built.

—Henry Pluckrose

Math Counts

Time

By Henry Pluckrose

Mathematics Consultant: Ramona G. Choos, Professor of Mathematics

Children's Press®

An Imprint of Scholastic Inc.

SCHOLASTIC

What do we mean by time?
Time is a measure of the hours, days, months, and years we live through.

What time do you go to school, have lunch, and go to bed?

We measure time so we can keep track of events.
We need to know what time a bus will come

and what time a train will leave the station.

We need to measure moments of time
to know how long things take.
How long does it take to boil
an egg so the yolk looks like this?

How do you make sure that toast does not burn?

We measure each day in hours from midnight. There are 12 hours from midnight to midday,

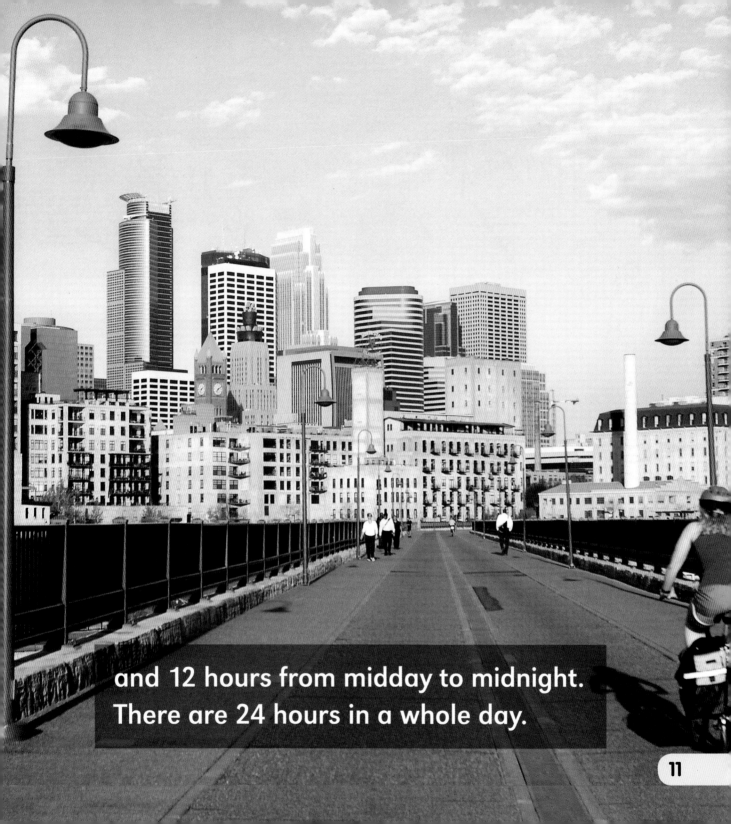

and 12 hours from midday to midnight.
There are 24 hours in a whole day.

Clocks measure time.
A clock has two hands.
The long hand marks the minutes.
The short hand marks the hours.

It takes 60 minutes for the long hand
to go around the clockface.
There are 60 minutes in each hour.

Smart Watch

10:12

Saturday, June 10

This is a digital watch.
Which number shows the hours?
Which number shows the minutes?

We measure short periods of time in seconds.
A special kind of watch is used to time a race.
The big hand measures seconds.
The small hand measures minutes.

The watch is started when the race begins. The watch is stopped when the winner crosses the finish line.

Longer periods of time are measured in weeks.
Seven days make one week.
On which day does the school week begin?

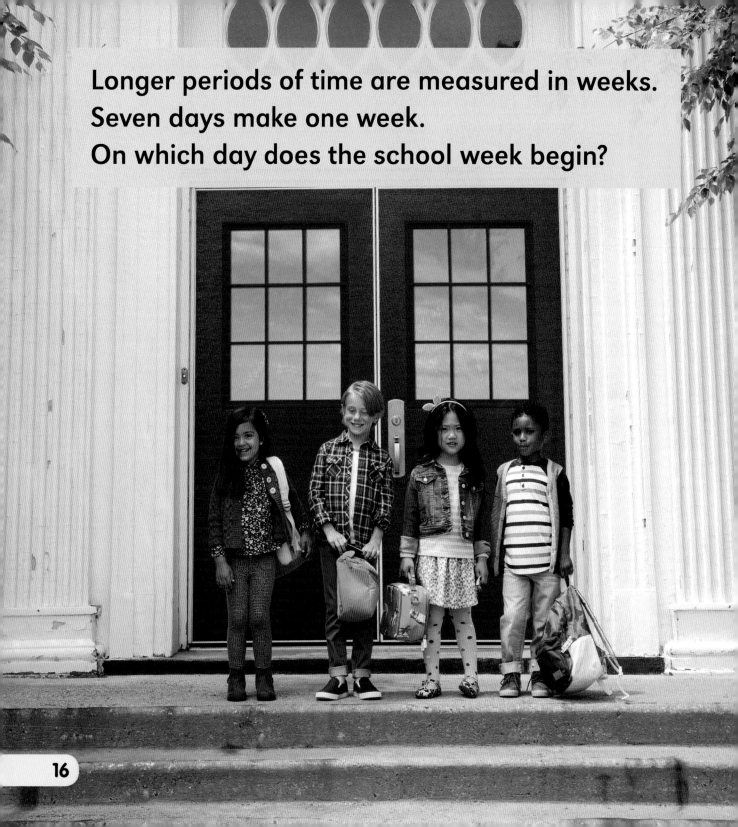

On which days do most people do their week's shopping?

ORGANIC BABY RED POTATOES $1.99 lb

ORGANIC ORANGE CAULIFLOWER $2.99 lb

Organic Cauliflower $2.99 lb

ORGANIC BOK CHOY $2.19 lb

ORGANIC NAPA CABBAGE $2.19 lb

ORGANIC BUTTERNUT SQUASH $1.99 lb

ORGANIC SPAGHETTI SQUASH $1.99 lb

Organic English Cucumber $3.69 ea

ORGANIC DAIKON $1.99 lb

ORGANIC RED POTATOES

ORGANIC BROCCOLI

A month is a longer period
of time than a week.
Some months last for 30 days
and some last for 31 days.
How is February different?
Winter months are often cold.

Summer months are often hot.
Some people go on vacation near the ocean.

Twelve months make one year.
On your first birthday,
you celebrated one year of life.

Everyone has birthdays.
This lady is enjoying a party
to celebrate her birthday.

21

We measure our age in years.
How old is the child who will have this cake?

We mark the passing of time in many other ways—by celebrating special holidays, such as New Year's Day,

by wearing special clothes,

or by watching fireworks.

Before people invented clocks,
they measured time with shadows

and even with candles.

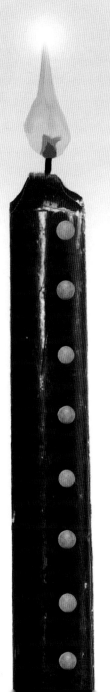

But a moving shadow or a burning candle does not give an exact measure of passing time. Planes have to fly on a timetable.

To catch a plane you need to be at the airport on time.
Otherwise the plane will take off without you.

There always has been time.
This castle was built many hundreds of years ago.
It is now a ruin.

These skyscrapers were built recently.
Long ago, even the castle was new and modern.

Index

Reader's Guide

Visit this Scholastic Web site to download the Reader's Guide for this series:
www.factsfornow.scholastic.com Enter the keywords **Math Counts**

Library of Congress Cataloging-in-Publication Data
Names: Pluckrose, Henry, 1931- author. | Choos, Ramona G., consultant.
Title: Time/by Henry Pluckrose; mathematics consultant: Ramona G. Choos, Professor of Mathematics.
Other titles: Math counts.
Description: Updated edition. | New York, NY: Children's Press, an imprint of Scholastic Inc., 2019. | Series: Math counts | Includes index.
Identifiers: LCCN 2017061281| ISBN 9780531175149 (library binding) | ISBN 9780531135235 (pbk.).
Subjects: LCSH: Time—Juvenile literature.
Classification: LCC QB209.5 .P58 2019 | DDC 529—dc23
LC record available at https://lccn.loc.gov/2017061281

Copyright © The Watts Publishing Group, 2018
Printed in Heshan, China 62

Scholastic Inc., 557 Broadway, New York, NY 10012.

2 3 4 5 6 7 8 9 10 R 28 27 26 25 24 23 22 21 20 19

Credits: Photos ©: 4: seanfboggs/iStockphoto; 5: monkeybusinessimages/iStockphoto; 6: shaunl/iStockphoto; 7: David Sailors/Getty Images; 8: MaraZe/Shutterstock; 8: ILYA AKINSHIN/Shutterstock; 9: Milos Luzanin/Shutterstock; 10: russellkord.com/age fotostock; 11: James Kirkikis/Shutterstock; 12: DougStevens/iStockphoto; 13: Alexey Boldin/Shutterstock; 14: Bormotov/Dreamstime; 15: Alistair Berg/Getty Images; 16: Kinzie Riehm/Getty Images; 17: ColorBlind/Getty Images; 18: Choreograph/iStockphoto; 19: FatCamera/iStockphoto; 20: Studio-Annika/iStockphoto; 21: Denis Raev/Dreamstime; 22: Liam Norris/Getty Images; 23: coward_lion/iStockphoto; 24: Alan Copson/Getty Images; 25: Pete Saloutos/Getty Images; 26: dbencek/iStockphoto; 27: Trevorl/Dreamstime; 28: PhotoAlto/Thierry Foulon/Getty Images; 29: Miguel Navarro/Getty Images; 30: Alexander Spatari/Getty Images; 31: VladimirSklyarov/iStockphoto.